KU-053-533

MARTHA OSPINA

Pergamano®

PARCHMENT CRAFT
BASIC TECHNIQUES

LA RIVIÈRE
CREATIEVE UITGEVERS

Pergamano® is the brand name under which books, materials and tools for the creative hobby Parchment Craft are marketed.

4th Edition, 1998

© 1997 La Rivière, creative publishers, Baarn, The Netherlands

Second Edition, 1998

All rights reserved. No part of this publication may be reproduced, stored in a retrieval system, published or transmitted, in any form or by any means, electronic, mechanical, photocopying, recording or ortherwise without prior written permission of the publisher.

ISBN 90 384 1247 9
NUGI 440

Photography: De Studio - fotografie + digitale beeldbewerking, Utrecht
Cover: Studio Jan de Boer, Vianen
Typesetting: Studio Imago, Amersfoort
Printing: Van der Weij bv grafische bedrijven, Hilversum

CONTENTS

1 PREFACE

You can learn the beautiful hobby Parchment Craft in many different ways.

One way is to follow a course from a Registered Pergamano Tutor*, another way is to teach yourself the various techniques by means of step-by-step pictures and instructions from this Pergamano book on basic techniques. The combination of both is even better: you can follow a course and also buy this book, then you will have two sources of information that will complement each other well. The choice is up to you.

This book is primarily made for beginners, but I am convinced many enthusiastic advanced Parchment Craft fans would want to have this book on their shelf.

The various techniques of Parchment Craft, like tracing, embossing, perforating, stippling and cutting, are all explained in a simple and clear way. Furthermore colouring techniques like dorsing and the use of Perga-Liner pencils are explained. Painting with the various Pergamano paints will be explained in the next Pergamano book, which is called: "Pergamano, Basic Techniques, Volume II".

The explanations in this book will be demonstrated by means of many clear step-by-step pictures. The book is easy to read: it is very easy to see from the pictures how the techniques should be done.
The text explains the technique in words and will reveal the tricks of the trade.

It is also a nice way to practise and you will immediately be able to make complete Pergamano projects such as a bookmark, a card with flowers, a card for Mother's Day, a Christmas card, etc.

This book is made with help from my Danish friend and Registered Pergamano Tutor Randi Hanson. She is a great lover of creative hobbies and since the introduction of Parchment Craft in Europe she has become a real expert in it. I would therefore like to thank Randi for her advice, her patterns and the finished projects for the pictures.

I would also like to thank the publisher, Anja Timmerman, for her co-operation during the preparations for this book and for its beautiful design. We have created many Pergamano books together. My thanks also goes to the photographic studio for the lay-out and beautiful quality of the pictures.

And now, dear reader, I wish you lots of success and fun with Parchment Craft. Are you a beginner? You will certainly be successful with the help of this book!

Should you have any comments on the book, please address the publisher.

Kind regards,

Martha Ospina

* For information about Registered Pergamano Tutors in your area please see page 63.

2 HISTORY OF PARCHMENT CRAFT

Parchment craft, to us a relatively new creative hobby, has in fact a fascinating history that goes back to the earliest days of written text.

The craft had its beginnings in religious art with religious or devotional pictures and communication cards. It began in Germany, Belgium and The Netherlands where the Catholic faith was strongest.

Until the 14th century the pictures were all hand drawn but by the 15th century printing was in its early stages and the images were cut in wood. Later they were engraved on copper plates and printing in large numbers became possible, first on parchment and later on hand made paper. In the beginning the pictures were only printed in black and white, and only very special ones would be coloured by hand.

At this time the pictures were mainly of Jesus suffering on the cross; of Saints; or other biblical texts in picture form.

As the art of printing developed and the demand for devotional pictures grew, more and more the production of these pictures had to be done mechanically just to keep up with demand. It was so much faster to print them than to draw them.

During the 18th century they started to print on larger pieces of parchment, and then to embellish a hand decorated border around the central figure or picture, thus bringing back a touch of the artist to the printed work. Again in this century they started to decorate around the pictures or at the edges of

Parchment card from round 1925

the cards with wavy cuts or perforations, initionally by hand but later by machines.

In very early days all the handwork was done by Monks, Nuns, and Novices, generally on real parchment. Strangely, even in those long gone days they were already working with the standard sizes we would recognise today as A4 or A5.

In the 19th century France, Paris especially, the pictures became more and more romantic and sweet. Lots of cherubs, young girl heads and flowers appeared on cards. They worked with relief and 3-dimensional effects, for instance a picture of a girl taking her first communion, and her dress would be made from real lace or tulle; cards were made with doors that could be opened , and other brilliant and beautiful ideas.

The beautifully perforated and decoratively cut borders were usually machine cut and then the cards were single, not opening cards. On the back would be a hand written wish or moral done in with a fine mapping pen in black ink.

The cards would be sent as tokens to friends and family in distant lands, including South America were the Catholic religion is widely spread. At the end of the last century, both in Europe and South America, the desire to make these cards by hand again surfaced. They used parchment, ordinary paper or parchment paper. They traced religious pictures, perforated and cut borders, and embossed a relief on the card. Frequently they cut a window out of the middle of the card and stuck in a picture or later a photograph.

It became popular to make communion cards for 15 year old girls, the age at which in many South American countries a girl is considered to become a woman – a very important occasion in a girl's life and it is celebrated in a grand way. Guests would make or buy a hand made card with the picture of a young woman in a sort of bridal gown, and they would write their greetings in it as we would today in birthday cards.

The end of the 19th century to today is not so long really. When I was a young girl in the sixties growing up in Colombia where I was born, I was taught to make cards from parchment paper during art classes at my Catholic school. They called it French technique, and no-one really knew why, but I guess its origin is in its history, all part of the romance of the craft.

Martha Ospina

3 PRESENTATION OF MATERIALS

Good quality material and tools are important for any art or hobby. It is more enjoyable to work with the proper tools and the result will be much better. In this book the materials and tools we used are Pergamano products. Pergamano is the brand name under which a large assortment of pattern packs, books and tools for the creative hobby parchment craft is being marketed in many countries all over the world. The manufacturer only occupies himself with parchment craft and regularly markets new books and materials.

In the picture you will see the materials and tools that are needed to make the projects of this book. Many other Pergamano products are available for example books with lots of patterns, patterns packs and paints. If you would like to receive more information about the various Pergamano products for parchment craft or about sales outlets, you can write to the following address: Marjo-Arte bv, P.O. Box 2288, 1180 EG Amstelveen, The Netherlands.

We will now describe the materials used:

Parchment paper:
Pergamano paper A4 (code 1481).
Pergamano paper is the basic material for Parchment Craft. All the examples in this book are made from this special paper.
One side of the Pergamano paper is smooth and the other side feels relatively rough.
Tracing is done on the rough side of the paper. Most of the embossing is done on the smooth side because the embossing tools have a better glide over this surface.
Be careful not to fold the paper too hard – it might crack.

Tools:
Embossing tool, small ball (code 1101).
Suitable for embossing small areas and thicker lines.

Embossing tool, large ball (code 1102).
Suitable for embossing large areas and for gentle embossing.

Embossing tool, fine stylus (code 1103).
Suitable for embossing fine lines and small details between perforations.

Embossing tool, extra fine ball (code 1107).
Suitable for embossing fine lines and decorative patterns between perforations.

1-needle tool (code 1104).
Suitable for embossing very thin lines, but is mostly used for perforating.

2-needle tool (code 1106).
Gives an even perforation suitable for cutting with the Pergamano scissors.

4-needle tool (code 1105).
Square shaped perforating tool for making the classic lace patterns.

3-needle tool (code 1108).
5-needle tool (code 1112).
Perforating tool suitable for making decorative and lace perforations.

Parchment scissors, Exclusive (code 1131).
Special shaped scissors for cutting the lace perforations.

Parchment scissors, stainless (code 1132).
Similar scissors with larger 'eyes' fit for bigger fingers.

Inks, colours:
White Tinta ink, 01T (code 1201).
White ink for tracing designs. Shake the bottle before use. As long as the ink is fluid, it can be thinned with water.

Gold Tinta ink, 22T (code1210).
Gold ink for tracing designs. Stir the bottle before use.

Tinta ink colours:
Suitable for tracing and painting. Look for other Pergamano books describing painting techniques with Tinta ink.

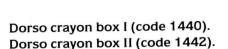

Dorso crayon box I (code 1440).
Dorso crayon box II (code 1442).
For colouring the reverse side of the paper. This 'easy to apply' colour gives the cards a soft tone that accentuates the embossed design.

Perga-Liners Box I (code 1451).
Water based coloured pencils for use on the front side of the cards.

Pads:
Felt embossing pad (code 1410).
To be used as a support when perforating with the 1 and 2 needle tool. Keep the plastic cover on. When it is damaged, replace it with a new transparent plastic bag.

Perforating pad, "Excellent", A5 (code 1419).
To be used as a support, when perforating with the 3, 4 and 5 needle tools.

Embossing pad, "De Luxe" (code 1413).
Soft even support for embossing with the different embossing tools. This black pad is easier to work on than the standard blue embossing pad, and is recommended for children.

Miscellaneous:
Mapping pen (code 1420).
The mapping pen is used for tracing with the Tinta inks.
The nip is kept inside the handle to prevent it from being damaged when not used.

Perga-Soft (code 1802).
A wax like product to ease embossing and perforations.

Paint /ink eraser (code 1423).
Pencil shaped eraser to rub off excess colour.

White colour pencil (code 9202).
Excellent for tracing straight outlines and folding lines. The white colour can also be applied to the reverse side of the paper to give areas a white appearance without embossing.

Other materials:
To make cards other materials or tools may be required, such as: adhesive tape, scissors for cutting paper, kitchen paper, small container for water, ruler, a piece of cardboard, hobby knife and cutting mat, paper clips, sewing needle, thin gold or sewing thread, different colours of thin paper (80g) for inserts, lavender oil, nylon tights, plastic stirrer or cocktails sticks.

4 TRACING

Tracing with Tinta white

The first step in any project is tracing, for this is the guide line for later work. With fine lines you mark out the areas that later are to be embossed or decorated.

A fine mapping pen is used for tracing. New pens can be greasy and reject the ink, so clean the tip in white spirit in order to remove any grease deposits. Tracing is done on the rough side of the paper, because the ink adheres more easily. When you fasten your parchment paper to the pattern with tape, remember to have the rough side upwards.

Shake the white Tinta ink before use. When filling the pen, dip only the tip of the nib into the ink. Do not dip the nib too far into the ink, otherwise you may have a mishap and drop some of the excess on to your work. The white ink is especially thick, and it does not require too much to draw several lines.

Hold the pen in an upright position to achieve very thin lines. Do not press the pen, let it glide over the paper. If the pressure is too hard the nib will open up and make thick lines or splashes. In the beginning it can be difficult to achieve very thin lines. It takes a little practice to achieve good results. Keep practising on a spare piece of paper, and you will succeed.

Draw the lines pulling the pen towards you. The pen will work better in this direction and it enables you to see more clearly where you are working. Whenever it is necessary, turn the paper to be able to trace the design lines towards yourself.

Always keep your pen completely clean. Before you re-fill the nib again, clean the nib in water and dry it with kitchen roll. Despite this precaution, it is still possible that the Tinta ink remains in the tip and therefore dry up. You may find it easier to have three mapping pens: one for white Tinta, one for gold Tinta, one for the coloured Tinta as these each have differing properties.

If you do make a small mistake, it is possible to remove the white ink with a razor blade (be careful it is very sharp!) or the Pergamano paint/ink eraser.

Tracing with gold/silver Tinta inks

These inks contain non-soluble metal pigments, so they are different to work with compared with the white ink.

Before use, shake the bottle and then roll it in your hand.

Because the pigments are heavy and sink to the bottom quickly, you should not dip the pen directly into the ink. Instead, dip a small cocktail stick in the ink and stir. Using the stick, place a small amount of the ink onto the nib.

The ink will now flow slowly down to the tip. Holding the pen vertically, gently start tracing. Do not put too much pressure on the pen in the beginning. Place a tiny spot of gold/silver before starting to trace the line, this makes it easier to get the flow of ink started.

5 EMBOSSING WITH THE SMALL BALL TOOL

Embossing enables one to make raised relief work in the parchment paper. Raising the design in this way, the colour of the parchment paper turns from light grey to satin white.

The small ball tool is excellent for embossing small areas such as flower petals and tiny leaves. It is also used to give curved outlines more effect.

Whenever you are embossing, you need a support underneath your parchment paper. The best embossing pad is the black "De Luxe" pad. It is soft, smooth and gives the best support for your paper. There is a smaller blue pad available which is also smooth, but it takes more pressure to do the embossing on this.

For children, this pad is excellent because they normally press very hard when they emboss.

Embossing is normally done on the back of the pattern, which is the smooth side of the paper. Place the parchment paper on the embossing pad with the design facing down. Gently rub the small ball tool backwards and forwards in parallel movements in the chosen area. You start the embossing with a slight downwards pressure so the paper can stretch. When you see the paper starting to become evenly white, you gradually increase the pressure until the paper becomes satin white. Be careful not to press too hard because the paper could tear. A well embossed area will have an even white satin-like colour and will contrast beautifully with the grey, almost translucent effect of the parchment paper.

When you emboss small dots, it is important to start working in the centre followed by a circular movement around the edge. If you only emboss using a circular movement, you could end up with a grey spot in the middle.

It is sometimes difficult to see the traced gold lines when working on the dark pad. Lay a sheet of kitchen paper between the pad and the parchment paper when you emboss gold lines. It helps you to see the gold lines more clearly.

It is not difficult to emboss nice reliefs in the paper, but it takes patience to achieve the even white satin-like colour. Do take your time.

Exercise A: Bookmark.

1: Cut out a piece of parchment paper so it fits the size of the bookmark. If you place correctly, it is possible to make 8 bookmarks out of one sheet of A4 paper. Use some small pieces of tape to fasten the parchment paper to the pattern. The smooth side of the parchment paper must be facing down towards the design.

2. Shake the white Tinta ink before tracing the flower petals, leaves, veins, the curved frames and the six groups of small ornaments between the frames. Hold the pen vertically to achieve thin white lines.

3. Shake the gold Tinta ink, and roll it between your hands. With a small cocktail stick, stir the gold before filling the mapping pen nib.

4. Trace the centres of the flowers and the small dots with gold. When the gold lines are dry, carefully remove the parchment paper from the pattern.

5. Place the bookmark with the tracing facing down on the soft part of the black embossing pad. Start embossing the flower petals with the small embossing ball. Emboss in parallel movements towards the centre. Sometimes you might wish to also emboss the petals outlines, to create a different effect. Remember to slowly increase the pressure. The petals should be very white. Emboss the leaves more gently to create a far less white effect than on the petals.
Emboss the ornaments with more pressure so they are very white

6. Emboss the small dot in the centre of the flowers just behind the gold spot. Emboss the small dots inside the frames. Start working in the centre followed by circular movements around the edge. If it is difficult to see the traced gold lines, lay a piece of kitchen paper between the pad and the parchment paper.
Finish the bookmark by rounding off the corners with scissors.

Congratulations! You have now finished your first piece of parchment craft. Use the bookmark to keep your place in this book.

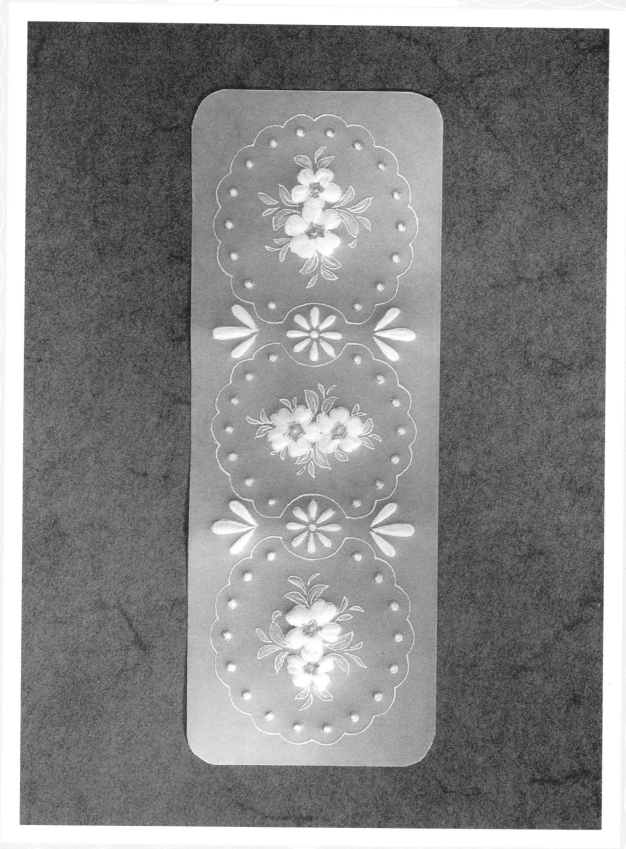

EXERCISE A: BOOKMARK

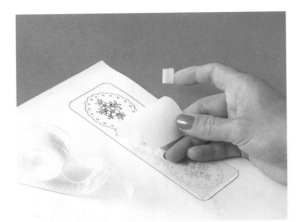

1. Fasten the parchment paper to the pattern.

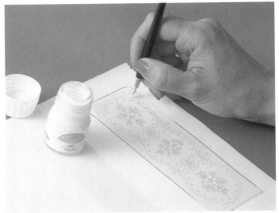

2. Hold the mapping pen in an almost vertical position.

3. Transferring gold ink on to the nib.

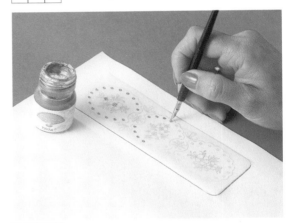

4. Tracing with gold ink.

5. Embossing of a petal.

6. Embossing of dots.

6 EMBOSSING WITH STYLUS

The stylus is excellent for embossing fine lines and small details.

Because of the small surface of the tool you need to apply only a very gentle pressure to obtain a thin white relief. Do be careful not to press too hard otherwise the stylus could damage the paper.

The stylus is used the same way as the small ball tool, it is important however to hold the stylus vertically during use because of the delicate tip.

The stylus is also used for a special hatching technique. In larger flower petals it gives a pleasing effect to emboss thin lines close together starting from the edge going towards the centre. The lines follow the direction of the veins and the embossing is done with a "press and lift" movement.

Exercise B, Card with flowers:

1. Place an size A5 piece of parchment paper on the pattern so the design is on the bottom half of the paper. The fold line should mark the middle of the paper. Trace the fold line with the white pencil using a ruler as support.

2. Trace with white Tinta: flower petals and the ornamental frame. Trace with gold Tinta: leaves, veins and stamens.

3. Place the card on the embossing pad and with the traced design facing down and using the stylus you now emboss fine lines in the petals. The direction is from the outside towards the centre. The lines are made with a "press and lift" movement so the lines are thicker towards the petals outlines. The lines are placed very close together because they should form the outline. Be careful not to press too hard. It is advisable to practise this technique on a spare piece of paper before starting on the card.

4. Emboss short lines with the stylus in the oblong ornaments. Use a ruler as support.
Emboss the small dots with the small ball tool.

5. Because the leaves are traced with gold, they should be embossed completely white. Use the reverse end of the tool to do a soft embossing on the leaves and in the flower centres. This will stretch the paper and give a good even base for when the embossing is continued with the small ball tool.

6. Emboss the leaves with the small ball tool in the lengthwise direction, but also follow the direction of the leaf outlines. Emboss the dots, and finally emboss the folding line with the small ball tool. Use a ruler as support.

7. Fold the card and find a piece of thin mint green paper to use as an insert. Fold the insert and put it inside the card. Hold the parchment paper and the insert together with paper clips. About 3 cm from the top and bottom line and with a sewing needle pierce two holes in the folding line. The holes should be about one centimetre apart. If you have the single needle tool, the piercing is done more easily with this.

8. Sew a gold or white thread through the pair of holes starting from the inside of one hole and through the hole one centimetre away, this time going from the outside and in. Tie the thread to a knot and then to a bow and cut the excess thread away. To complete the card, cut off the excess paper if necessary.

EXERCISE B: CARD WITH FLOWERS

1. Tracing the folding line.

2. The traced card.

 3. The 'press and lift' movement.

 4. The embossing of fine lines.

5. Embossing with the back of the embossing tool.

 6. Close-up of the embossed flowers.

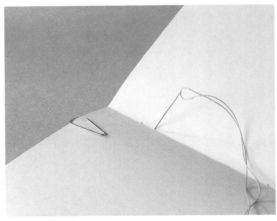

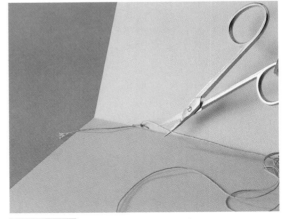

7. Piercing holes in the card and insert.

 8. Cutting the thread.

7 DORSING

Dorsing means colouring with a Dorso crayon.

The crayons are easy to use and the soft colours match the paper and accentuate the embossed designs.

The Dorso crayons are normally applied to the reverse side of the paper so that the designs can be embossed white.

Dorsing a sheet of paper.

Instead of using the parchment paper as it is, it is possible to colour the paper before using it for a card. It will give the cards a completely different look. The colouring is done before the tracing.

1. Place the parchment paper with the smooth side upwards on a hard and smooth surface i.e. a piece of cardboard. Use the flat end of the crayon to rub evenly on the paper. Use either just one colour or for varying effects two or even three colours. For this example magenta, blue and violet is used in diagonal stripes.

2. Fold a piece of kitchen paper or old nylons; put one drop of lavender oil or any other fine oil on it.

   With the kitchen paper the colours are now evened out and the excess colour removed. Rub firmly, holding the parchment paper in place with your other hand.

   Spread the stripe of the first colour then change the kitchen paper before spreading the next colour. The third colour is also spread the same way.

3. Finally the colours are blended together by working the areas between the stripes.

4. The dorsed paper is now ready for tracing. Place it on the design with the dorsed side of the paper facing down. Hold the parchment to the design with some small pieces of tape, this time with the rough side up. The tracing is done as usual.

Using a hairdryer.

Instead of using lavender oil, you can heat up the crayons on the parchment paper before spreading the colours with kitchen paper. Hold the hairdryer almost against the Dorso on the parchment paper. After a few seconds the wax in the colour will start to melt and the soft crayons are easy to even out. With this technique you are able to get a stronger colour for the finished result.

Dorsing used in smaller areas.

Instead of dorsing a whole sheet of parchment paper, Dorso is often used in small defined areas or as a soft background behind a design. In the following exercises you will be able to try different ways of using the Dorso crayons.

Repeating exercise A and B:

Colour a sheet of A4 parchment paper with Dorso crayons using magenta, blue and violet. Make diagonal stripes.

Repeat the exercise A and B.

You will find that the result looks completely different from before because of the colour. You now have more knowledge of the paper, so your embossing should now be whiter.

DORSING A PIECE OF PARCHMENT PAPER

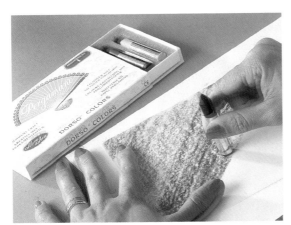

1. Applying Dorso crayons.

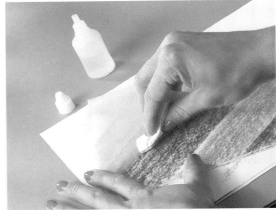

2. Spreading the Dorso crayon by rubbing.

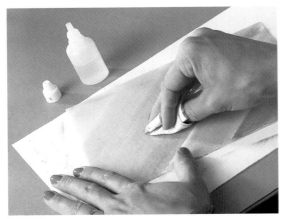

3. The blending of the colours.

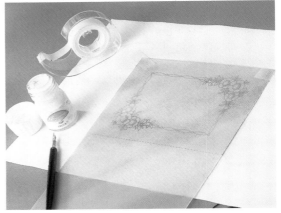

4. Place the dorsed paper on to the pattern.

8 EMBOSSING WITH LARGE BALL TOOL

This tool is used for embossing larger areas and creating lighter effects. Because of its size it is quicker to use than the small ball tool and the embossing is more even. You cannot achieve the same whiteness with this tool, so if the area has to be completely satin white you must continue embossing with the small ball.

For very large areas one should first emboss with the reverse end of the tool. Using the plastic end, the paper will slowly start to stretch, and this gives a good foundation for further embossing.

When the paper has stretched you should continue embossing with the metal tool again. You should be moving the tool back and forwards in parallel movements. Very slowly increase the pressure until you have achieved a soft whiteness. If you wish the area to be more white, there are two things you can do: 1) Shade the area with the white colour pencil. This is done on the same side as the embossing. 2) Continue embossing with the small ball tool, but on very large areas this must be done very

carefully otherwise the parchment paper will tear or the embossing will be uneven.

On smaller areas such as flower petals it is easier and quicker to start the embossing with the large ball tool and then to continue with the small ball tool.

Exercise C, Ship:

1. Place a size A5 piece of parchment paper on the pattern so the design is on the bottom half of the paper. Trace the folding line with the white pencil using a ruler as support.
   Trace with gold Tinta: Ornaments in corners.
   Trace with white Tinta ink the rest of the design.
2. Use Dorso crayons on the reverse side to colour the water and sky .
   Water: The Dorso violet and blue crayons are rubbed on the water in horizontal lines. Spread the colours with a piece of kitchen paper. Because the Dorso has to stay inside the oval frame, the kitchen paper is folded to a point,

this gives a finer point and better control when spreading the colour. If the Dorso colour should go outside the frame, it is easily removed with the Pergamano ink eraser.

3. Sky: Blue Dorso is applied on the area just above the water. With a folded piece of kitchen paper the blue colour is toned out, so the top part of the sky is very pale blue. Remember to colour the small areas under the sails.

4. Place the card on the embossing pad with the traced design facing down. Emboss the sails with the reverse end of the embossing tool and when the paper has started to stretch continue the embossing with the large ball tool. Because of the size of the sails the pressure of the embossing must be increased very slowly. It takes patience to get the larger areas an even white. Separate the three small sails by embossing more on the parts that overlap.

If you are not satisfied with the white on your embossed area, then use the small ball tool.

5. Emboss the mast, the flag and a few small waves with the small ball tool. Emboss the boat very gently with the large ball tool. Emboss the spaces between the double gold lines in the oval framing the boat.

Use the large ball to emboss between the double outlines, embossing one section at a time and gently working your way around. If you split the long section up in 2 or 3 parts, the embossing will become uneven. The longer the movements with the tool, the better the result will be. Work in the same way with the small ball tool to make the frame whiter.

To complete, fold the card and insert a piece of blue paper inside.

EXERCISE C: SHIP

1. Close-up of the traced card.

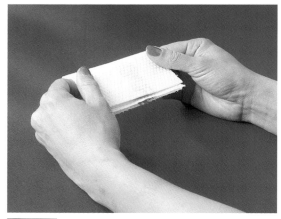

2a. Folding kitchen paper.

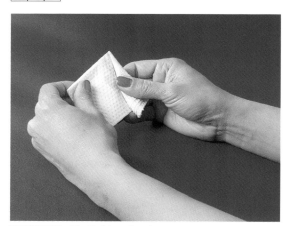

2b. Folding kitchen paper to a point.

3. Dorsing the sea.

4. Embossing the sails.

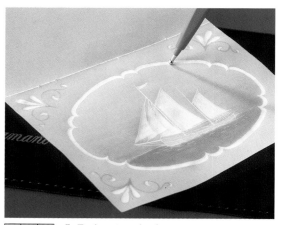

5. Embossing the frame.

9 STIPPLING

Stippling is a type of gentle hammering, giving a matt white surface. By stippling parts of the design, the surface of the card is varied. This makes the card more interesting to look at.

Stippling is done on the reverse side of the paper.

First the area is gently embossed with the large ball tool (use the black pad as support). Place the card with the traced design face down on a piece of dark cardboard. Perforate small holes with the single needle whilst holding the tool in a vertical position. The single needle will not really make holes because of the hard cardboard, but it will create small white dots on the front side. Place these 'dots' very close together to give the matt white appearance. After this is completed, the area can be gently coloured with the white pencil on both sides.

White traced lines can also be stippled for a different effect. Here you must be careful not to place the holes too close together otherwise the paper could crack along the line. These lines should not be coloured with the white pencil.

10 EMBOSSING WITH SINGLE NEEDLE

Very thin lines can be embossed with the single needle tool. Different from the other embossing tools, the single needle should not be held vertically during embossing. It should be used at an angle of approximately 45 degrees.

Because of the limited pressure that can be applied with this tool, the embossed lines are not completely white.

Curved lines should be made in free hand, but straight lines should be embossed using a ruler as support.

Embossing without tracing.

If very fine embossed lines are needed, they are not traced with ink on the parchment paper because it is very difficult to trace such fine lines. Instead, the lines can be obtained using the one needle tool while the parchment paper is attached to the pattern. Place the parchment paper with the pattern on to the embossing pad, and gently emboss a fine line with the single needle tool as indicated on the design.

11 PERFORATING WITH SINGLE NEEDLE

Perforations can be used as decoration or as part of the process of removing pieces of parchment paper e.g. along curved outlines.

When perforating with the single needle tool, it is important that you keep the cardboard beneath your felt pad, as without the cardboard the long needle can go through the felt pad and damage the table beneath.

When used as decoration, the perforations can be done from both sides of the parchment paper, depending on which effect is wanted. If a lot of dots are embossed on a design it gives a nice effect to pierce a hole through the centre of each dot. This is normally done from the front side.

Perforating curved outlines

Many Pergamano designs have curved outlines, as this gives a more lace-like impression to the finished result.
In order to give the curved outlines a nicer appearance they should be separated from the excess paper by perforating with the single needle tool. These cards are often mistaken for lace or embroidery.

Before perforating, the traced outlines are embossed with the small ball tool. The card is then placed on the felt pad with the traced side upwards. Holes are pierced through the front side with the single needle, just outside the embossed edge of the card. When using the single needle tool it should always be held in a vertical position, and the needle must go deep down into the felt pad. The holes should be placed very close together so the excess paper is easily separated from the curved outline. This can be done by pressing down your thumbnail just beside the perforation, or by embossing with the large ball tool on the outer part of the perforation. Please note that perforations are normally indicated on the patterns with small dots.
When you are making a double card with an insert, the card should be folded and the insert sewn to it before perforating through the 4 layers of paper. To make this perforating easier, the tip of the sin-

gle needle may be coated with a little Perga-Soft. This helps the needle glide more freely though the multiple layers of paper. The excess paper is removed one sheet of paper at a time. Do not try to do all sheets at the same time.

Exercise D, Star:

1. Because of the curved edges, the size of the Pergamano paper must be 17 x 23 cm. The rule is to leave at least 5 mm of excess paper outside the curved outlines. Trace the outline with gold Tinta and also the inner star figures in each star. With the exception of the straight lines in the stars, the rest of the design is traced with white Tinta.
2. Place the card (still taped to the pattern) on to the embossing pad and emboss all the beams in the stars with the single needle tool. Use a ruler as support and, starting from the centre, emboss towards the outline. Where the embossing starts you will need to press slightly harder.
3. Remove the card from the pattern and colour on the reverse side the stars with yellow Dorso. Avoid the double curved outlines on the 3 large stars. Spread the colour with a rolled tip of kitchen paper. Apply a little Dorso fuchsia along the outlines of the yellow dorsed area in the 3 large stars.
   Spread the fuchsia colour to blend it into the yellow. Use the Pergamano ink eraser to remove excess Dorso.
   Emboss the 10 lentil shaped figures around each large star softly with the large ball tool. Place the card on a piece of cardboard with the traced design facing downwards. Stipple small holes inside the lentil shaped figures. First perforate the outlines with small dots before filling the figures with tiny holes. End the stippling process by colouring the perforated areas with white colour pencil.
4. Emboss the small gold traced stars with the large ball embossing tool followed by the small ball tool. Emboss the white traced line just beside the inner gold star with the small ball tool. Also use the small ball tool when embossing the small dots along the edge and behind the golden outline.

Close-up:
Perforations made
with one needle tool.

Turn the paper and perforate a hole in the middle of each embossed dot with the single needle tool, using the felt pad as support. Perforate small holes in the white curved line and around the embossed dots, be careful not to place the dots too close.

5. Fold the card and sew in an insert of pink coloured paper. Place the card on the felt pad with the tracing face up. Hold the card together with paper clips. Perforate outside the embossed gold line, making the holes deep and close together.

6. Remove the excess paper one sheet at a time by pressing down with the thumbnail on the outer part of the perforations.

EXERCISE D: STARS

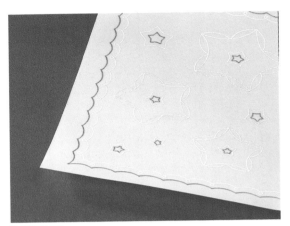

1. Close-up of the traced pattern.

2. Embossing with the single needle tool.

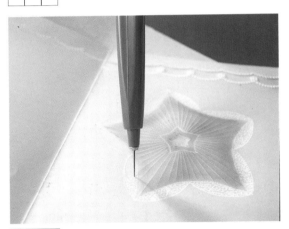

3. Close-up of stippling.

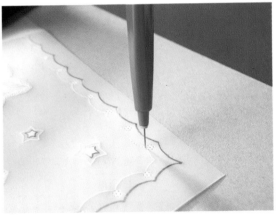

4. Stippling the white contours of the card.

5. Perforating along the contours.

6. Removing excess paper.

12 PERFORATING WITH 3- AND 5 NEEDLE TOOL

We are now ready to introduce simple lace patterns. For this purpose the 3- and 5 needle tools are ideal. They are easy to use and together with fine embossing you are able to create delicate lace works.

When perforating with these tools you need to use the "Excellent" perforation pad, as this will give better support than the felt pad. It is especially important when working with multi-needle tools, to have a firmer more stabile support, otherwise the paper tends to crack during perforating.

Patterns with the 3- and 5 needle tools are indicated with blocks of small black dots. Look at the next pattern (exercise E), where the "Best Wishes" card has work requiring the 3-needle tool. The other pattern has lace work requiring the 5-needle tool.

The position of the 3- and 5-needles must be very precise, so it is necessary to perforate with the pattern underneath the Pergamano paper. To avoid spoiling your original pattern, I suggest you make one photocopy of the pattern for your own use, and perforate on that.

The lace work is done in 4 stages:

1. Place the card and the photocopied pattern on the "Excellent" perforation pad. Perforate gently with the tool as indicated on the pattern. By 'gently' we mean that only the tips of the needles pass through the Pergamano paper, and do not go too deeply into the pattern. The soft perforation leaves the Pergamano paper strong enough to be embossed around and between the holes.
2. Separate the pattern and the card. Place the card on the embossing pad, and emboss between the holes. This is normally done with the stylus or the extra small embossing tool.
3. Place the card on the 'Excellent' perforating pad with the tracing facing upwards. Perforate again, but this time do a deep perforation. The points of the needles may vary, so I recommend that you mark the tool to enable you to hold it in the same position every time.
4. Instead of taking the tool totally out, the needles

are left with the points just inside the Pergamano paper. Twist the tool a little to the left and then to the right, to make the holes bigger and oval before withdrawing completely from the paper.

Exercise E: Best Wishes:

1. Size of paper: 148 mm x 105 mm (A6).
   Trace the outline and the text with gold Tinta ink. Place the card and the pattern on the "Excellent" pad. Perforate gently with the 3-needle tool as indicated on the pattern.
2. Separate the card from the pattern. On the reverse side, emboss a small dot in the middle of each 3 needle perforation using the extra small ball embossing tool. Emboss a large dot in the

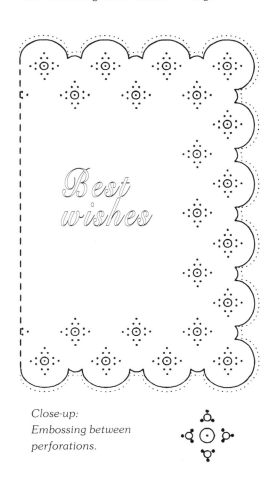

Close-up:
Embossing between
perforations.

centre of each group of perforations. Make the embossing harder than indicated on the "close-up" picture. Emboss the gold outline and the text with the extra small ball.

3. Place the card on the "Excellent" perforating pad and perforate deeply with the 3-needle tool.
4. Leave the tip of the tool in the Pergamano paper. Twist a little to the left and right to make oval holes. Using the single needle tool, perforate a hole in the centre of the large embossed dots. Fold the card and insert a folded piece of dark red coloured paper. Using paper clips, keep the red paper in position between the folded sheets. Perforate outside the gold line with the single needle tool. Remove the excess paper.

Small card :

1. Size of paper: 148 mm x 105 mm (A6).
   Trace the outline with gold Tinta and perforate gently with the 5-needle tool as indicated on the pattern.
2. Emboss a circle around the centre hole with the extra small ball tool. Emboss a fine line around the group of 5-needle perforations with the stylus. Look at the "close-up" explanation to see the steps of the embossing. Emboss as indicated the small dots in the curved parts of the outline.
3. Perforate deeply. Lift the 5-needle tool and make a tiny twist movement to create 4 oval holes round the centre.
   Fold the card and insert a folded piece of violet coloured paper. Hold the card together with paper clips and perforate outside the gold line with the single needle tool. Remove the excess paper.

Close-up:
Embossing between per-
forations.

1

2

3

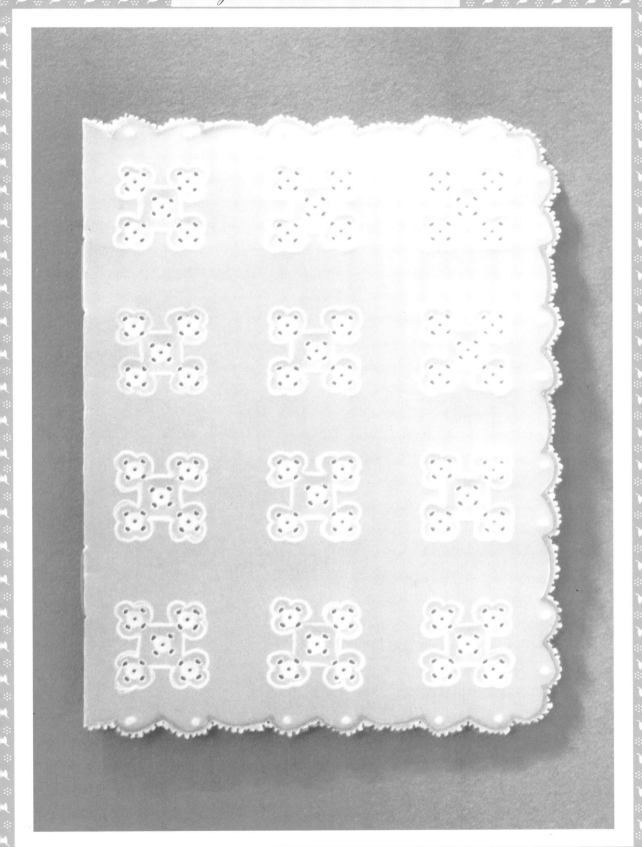

EXERCISE E: BEST WISHES

 1. Marking the perforations with the 3-needle tool.

2. Embossing between the perforations.

3. Perforating deeply with the 3-needle tool.

4. The twisting of the 3-needle tool in order to make oval holes.

EXERCISE E: SMALL CARD

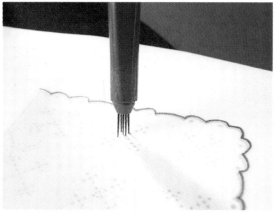

1. Marking the perforations with the 5-needle tool.

2. Embossing around the perforations using the fine stylus.

3. The twisting of the 5-needle tool.

13 PERFORATING WITH 2-NEEDLE TOOL

The 2-needle tool is used when you wish to perforate and cut out parts of the parchment paper. Compared with the single needle tool, this tool leaves a better and more even perforated edge, suitable for cutting with the Pergamano scissors.

When using the 2-needle tool, the first perforation will leave two holes in the paper. The second and subsequent perforations will only leave one new hole as you use the second hole of the last perforation to carry out the next perforation. This way you ensure all the perforations are the same distance apart. The edge now will be suitable for cutting with the Pergamano scissors. You require the felt pad as support as you did with the single needle tool. Perforations must be deep, so the hole will be wide enough to fit the points of the scissors.

Cutting with the Pergamano scissors

If you want the best results when using the Pergamano scissors, they have to be held in a special way that will probably require some practice.

Place the Pergamano scissors in your left hand with the blades downwards. Insert the index finger of your right hand in the left eye and the middle finger into the right eye. Place the scissors in the first bend of the fingers and rest the thumb against the left eye of the scissors.

The distance between the perforations of the 2-needles are 1 mm, so this should also be the distance between the tip of the blades, before they are inserted into the perforations. Do not press the tip of the blades too deeply into the perforations, otherwise you will make the holes too large. While cutting, the blades are turned slightly to the left, to achieve a better result. The angle between the scissors and the paper should be as shallow as possible in order to form the special picot edge.

Some people place the card on the felt pad when cutting, while others prefer to hold the work over the index finger of the left hand. Try both ways, and choose the one that you prefer.

Exercise F, Mother's day:

1. Paper size: 233 mm x 167 mm.
   Trace the flowers, leaves and curved outline with white Tinta. Use gold Tinta to trace the heart and the text. Mark the folding line and the top line of the card with white pencil.

2. Use Dorso fuchsia in the small heart.
   Apply Dorso violet around the heart, the flowers and behind the text. For additional highlights, apply a little Dorso fuchsia around the heart and between the two lines of text.
   Place the Pergamano paper again on the design and perforate gently with the 5-needle tool.
   In the large flower petals first emboss the lines with the stylus followed by the extra small ball tool. The embossing starts from the point of the petal and goes towards the centre. Emboss the small flowers, making the petals completely white. The leaves are embossed gently with both the large and small ball tools.
   Between the double gold lines of the heart and text, emboss with the large and small ball tool:
   the curved outline, the small dots along side, the circle and small dots between the five needle perforations as well as the centres of all the flowers are embossed using the extra small ball tool.
   Turn the card over and make deep perforations from the front side with the 5-needle tool. Leave the tip of the tool in the Pergamano paper and twist it a little to the left and right to make oval holes. Start perforating with the 2-needle tool as indicated on the pattern.

3. Cut between the perforations with the Pergamano scissors until the excess paper falls off. Remember to keep the angle between the scissors and the paper as shallow as possible.
   Fold the card and insert a piece of rainbow coloured paper. Perforate outside the curved outline with the 2-needle tool, then cut the top edge of the card using a rule and a hobby knife. Remove the excess paper.

To Mum

Close-up of the embossing of dots along the outlines.

Close-up of the embossing between the perforations.

EXERCISE F: MOTHER'S DAY

 1. The traced pattern.

2. Perforating with the 2-needle tool.

 3. The position of the fingers while cutting.

 4. Cutting the 2-needle perforations.

14 MAKING LACE WORK – 4-HOLE COMBINATIONS

This delicate lace work is one of the great hallmarks of the craft. By perforating and cutting away parts of the paper you will be able to create beautiful designs that look like lace.

The making and cutting of 4-hole combinations takes time and patience, but the unique result is worth the effort.

Perforating with the 4-needle tool.

Because this tool has many needles, for best results the "Excellent" perforating pad is recommended as a base on which to work.

As with the three-needle tool, the work is done in several steps:

1. Place the card and the photocopied pattern on the perforation pad. Perforate gently with the tool following the pattern.
   Four holes in a group indicates a cross. A combination of two 4 four hole groups indicates a slot. When perforating the slots, you begin by perforating the four holes in the centre of the line, then you work to the sides. Two of the needles must go into two already perforated holes, and the other two will give a new perforation. In this way, the distance between the holes/groups will be the same.
2. Separate the pattern and the card. Place the card on the embossing pad, and emboss between the holes. This is normally done with the stylus or the extra small embossing tool.
3. Place the card on the "Excellent" perforation pad with the tracing facing upwards. Perforate again, but this time do a deep perforation. The shapes of the four-needle tools can be slightly different. To ensure that you get the tool entering the holes in exactly the same way as when you made your first perforation, you should mark the tool so that you always hold it the same way round.

Cutting crosses with the Pergamano scissors

The scissors are held again in the same way as described in the paragraph "Cutting with the Pergamano scissors".

1. Turn the Pergamano paper so the 4-hole group is square to you. Insert the scissors into the top holes of the group. While cutting, turn the scissors slightly to the left. Be careful not to insert the blades too deeply into the paper, this would make the holes too large.
   The angle between the scissors and the paper should be as shallow as possible to form the V-shape cutting.
2. Turn the Pergamano paper 90 degrees to the left. Cut again between the top holes in the group.
3. Repeat part 2.
4. Finally turn the paper 90 degrees to the left again, then cut the last part of the hole. You should now have a cross-like hole.

Cutting slots with the Pergamano scissors

A slot is cut in four steps like the cross. You cut between the top hole on all sides of the group, working from the left to right. This will create the oblong hole known as a slot.

Exercise G, Lace bookmark:

1. Paper size: 52 mm x 148 mm.

1.Tracing:

Using gold Tinta, trace the outline, the square figure, and the ornaments.

Perforating:

Perforate gently with the 3-, 4- and 5-needle tools as indicated on the pattern.

2. Embossing:

Using the extra small ball tool emboss the outline; the inside of the gold ornaments; the small dot in

*The lace bookmark:
close-up of the embossing
between the perforations.*

the middle of the 3-needle perforation; the large and 4 small dots between the 5-needle perforation and finally the small dots in the space between the 4-needle perforations.

3. Perforating:

Perforate deeply with the 3- and 5-needle tools and give the needles a twist to create oval holes as explained previously. Perforate deeply with the 4-needle tool.

4. Cutting:

Place the bookmark so the perforations are square to you. Start cutting the top sets of holes in each four hole perforation with the Pergamano scissors.

5. Turn the book mark 90 degrees to the left and cut the top set of holes in each four hole perforation.

6. Repeat step five.

7. Finally for the fourth time turn the bookmark and cut the last top set of holes. You should now have cross-shaped holes between the embossed dots.

Finishing off:

Perforate outside the outlines with the 2-needle tool and cut the excess paper off with the Pergamano scissors.

'We've moved' card:

1: Paper size: A4.

Tracing:

Using gold Tinta ink, trace the text and the gate (not the dots between the perforations). Use white Tinta to trace the plants and butterflies.

Dorsing:

On the reverse side apply Dorso fuchsia in the centre of the flower, and Dorso violet for the petals. Use Dorso yellow ochre for the gate and a little Dorso blue for the sky.

Perforating:

Perforate the 4-hole combinations gently.

Embossing:

Flowers: Use the extra small ball tool to emboss the very short lines going from the outline towards the centre. Emboss a few long lines. Make small dots in the centre.

Leaves: Emboss on one side of the leaf on the outside edge using the large ball tool. On the other half, emboss along the centre vein, then gently along the outside edge. Press a little harder along the outline and the vein so the embossing has different shades.

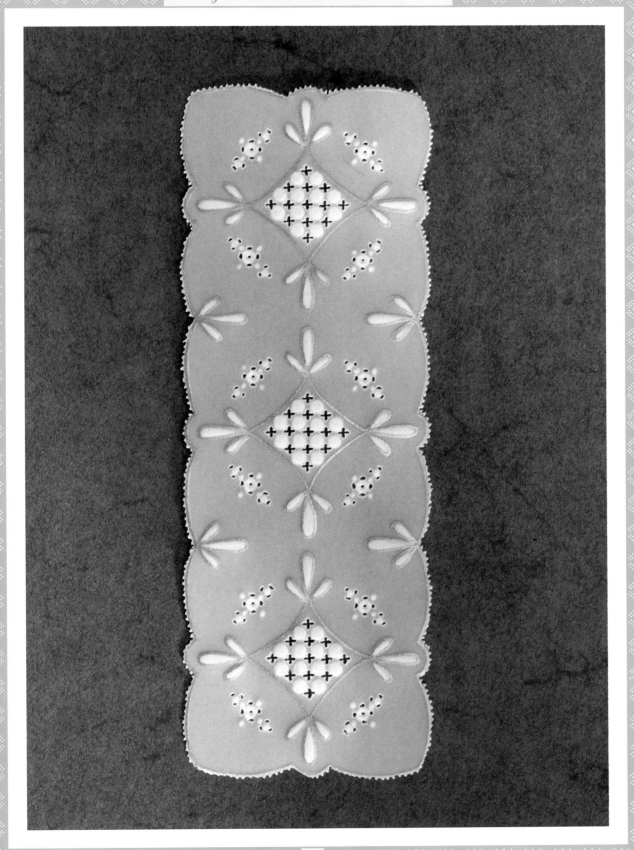

House Warming Party

I've Moved

We've Moved

Gate: Emboss the hearts with the small ball tool. With the extra small ball tool emboss the small dots; the ovals and the text.

Butterflies: Emboss the wings and bodies using the extra small ball tool.

2. Perforating:

Perforate the 4-hole combinations deeply with the 4-needle tool.

Cutting:

Cut the 4-hole combinations to form crosses and slots.

Finishing off:

Fold the card and insert a pink coloured paper.

EXERCISE G: LACE BOOKMARK

1. Marking the perforations with the 4-needle tool.

2. Embossing with the extra fine embossing tool.

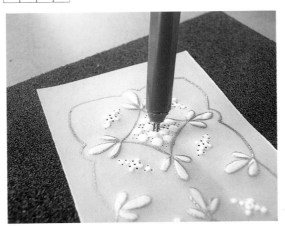

3. Perforating deeply with the 4-needle tool.

4. The cutting: step 1.

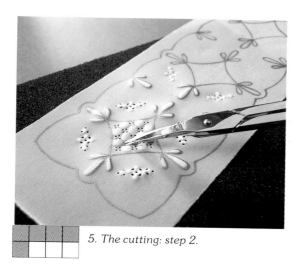

5. The cutting: step 2.

6. The cutting: step 3.

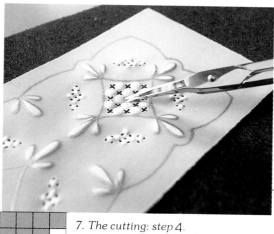

7. The cutting: step 4.

EXERCISE G: WE'VE MOVED!

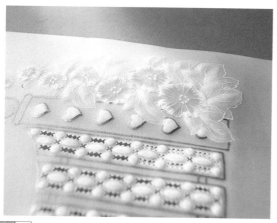

1. Close-up of the embossing.

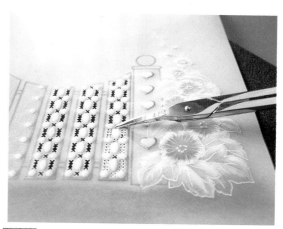

2. The cutting of slots.

15 SIMPLE PAINTING WITH PERGA-LINERS (BOX II)

The Perga-Liners from Box II are water compatible coloured pencils, especially chosen for working with Pergamano paper. The box contains a range of soft colours, that match the tone of the paper.

White traced designs with one colour decoration:

After tracing, the Pergamano paper is removed from the pattern so the black lines do not distract you when painting. The Pergamano paper is then placed on a sheet of coloured paper so the white traced lines are visible more easily.

The simplest way of using the Perga-Liner pencils is to make thin lines along-side the white traced ornament or outlines. One or two coats of colour can be painted on the front side, depending on how dark a shade is wanted. Try to avoid painting on the traced line because the white embossed lines are an important part of this decoration.

Colouring of larger areas is also done by painting lines. The pencil is used with a "press and lift movement". It is like using the pencil as a paint brush, When the line is started, the pencil is pressed gently to make the line thicker, then using less pressure you taper the stroke enabling the line to become very thin. This also ensures that the darkest shade of the colour is at the beginning of the line.

To build up different shades in the design, it is always important to make the lines in the correct direction. The lines must always start on the area where the darker shade is required. The first coat of colour is made with the longest strokes, the next with shorter, and finally the third layer with very short strokes. This can be repeated if darker shades are wanted.

Often, when many layers of colour are painted, a little excess colour will appear on the surface of the card. Just blow this away to prevent colour stains from spoiling your work.

Exercise H, Butterflies.

1. Paper size: 148 mm x 296 mm.

Tracing:
Using gold Tinta, trace the outline; the ornamental frame around the four hole combinations; the small dots; the body and also the antennas of the butterflies.

With white Tinta trace the rest of the card (but not the figures between the four-hole combinations).

Painting:
Remove the Pergamano paper from the pattern and apply the colours on the front side using:

PL A6 light violet for the line inside the scrolls (just beside the traced line) and

PL A4 blue for inside the white outline of the card.

PL A3 black for the body of the butterflies and now PL A6 light violet in the points of the ornament in the corners. Starting from the point, let the lines follow the figure and let them end towards the centre of it. Apply 3 times with differing lengths of strokes. From the outlines of the buttlerfly wings apply the PL A4 blue and decorate using 3 layers of colour.

Perforating:
Perforate gently with the 3-needle tool as indicated on the pattern.

Perforate the four hole combinations gently with the 4-needle tool.

Embossing:
4-hole combinations: Because the pattern within the 4-hole combinations is more complicated this time, the outlines of the figures are traced with the stylus before embossing with the extra small ball tool.

First make the dots, then the flowers.

Emboss inside the gold ornaments surrounding the 4-hole combinations.

Butterflies: Emboss the outlines of the wings and the ornaments with the extra small ball. Emboss some small dots on the outside of the pointed parts of the wings.

Scrolls and gold dots: Emboss the white traced scrolls and the gold dots with the extra small ball tool.

Corner figures: Use the stylus to emboss the lines following the shape of the figure. Emboss both the gold and white outlines with the extra small ball tool.

Perforating:

Perforate with the 3-needle tool again, this time deeply, and twist it to create oval holes.
Using the 4-needle tool, again perforate deeply.

Cutting:

Cut the 4-hole combinations into crosses and slots.

Finishing off:

Fold the card and insert a sheet of lavender blue paper. Perforate the outline with the 1- or 2-needle tool and remove the excess paper.

EXERCISE H: BUTTERFLIES

1. Making thin lines with Perga-Liners.

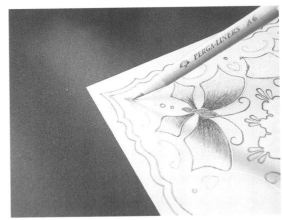

2. Colouring the decorations in the corners.

3. Colouring the butterflies.

4. Embossing the flowers with the stylus.

16 TRACING WITH COLOURED INK

There are many coloured Tinta inks, and when tracing with these you can obtain colourful effects when parts, or even the whole design, is traced.

It is important to use just a little of the coloured Tinta ink on your nib, as they are not as thick as the white or gold inks. It is important to avoid hard pressure on the pen, otherwise the traced lines will be too thick.

Mixing 2 and 3 colours of Perga-Liners.

When a realistic effect is required, for example more shades of red are needed than available in the box, the desired shades can be obtained by mixing existing colours.

In the one colour technique, the 'shades' are created using gentle lines. It is important that the lines follow the natural shape of the figure or plant etc..

Applying the colour is done in two stages:
1: The first layer of colour is used for making highlights and shadows. These colours only cover parts of the areas.

2: Next, the basic colour will be painted – also in lines, so it blends in with the darks shades and the highlights. Take care that the highlight areas do not become too dark.

Embossing behind Perga-Liners.

Because the Perga-Liners stay on top of the paper, some of the grains will disappear during the embossing. With the whitening of the paper and the less grains, the embossed areas will appear lighter. In this way we create a more marked 'highlight'.

When a 'dry' painting is done with the Perga-Liners, only the highlighted areas should be embossed.

Exercise I, Pansy:

1. This is an 'envelope' card, which means that the card has been folded twice. Look at the illustrations of the unfolded card. It gives an indication of where to place the flowers and perforations.

Tracing:

White colour pencil: Start at one end of the Pergamano paper and mark the two squared parts

Using PL A19 yellow, shade in the three lower petals of the flower and the small petals in the buds.

For highlighting the leaves, use PL A15 leaf green, then PL A14 for the darker shading.

2. Second coat of Perga-Liners:

Flowers: Colour the two top petals of the flower and the large petals of the bud with PL A6 light violet. Colour the centre and the remaining petals with PL A20 light yellow, and for the veins use PL A7 violet.

For the leaves and stalks use PL A13 light green, and the flower heart PL A14 green.

Apply a line of PL A7 violet along the inner rim of the single white outline as well as inside the small triangles.

Perforating:
Perforate the 4-hole combinations gently.

Embossing:
With the extra small ball tool emboss the curved edge, the gold ornaments, the single white line and between the curved double white lines. Emboss around the 4-hole combinations and also the contours of the triangles and small dots.

Emboss the highlights of the flowers, inside the petals and between the lines, working from the edge towards the centre. Use the small ball and then the large ball tool to soften the lines. Emboss the pollen with the small ball tool.

Leaves: emboss the highlighted area with the small ball or the large ball tool depending on the size of the leaf. In the large leaves only use a little pressure between the veins.

Perforating:
Make deep perforations with the 4-needle tool and perforate with the 2-needle inside the curved bows as indicated on the pattern. Also perforate outside the curved edge.

Cutting:
Cut the four hole combinations into slots.
Cut between the 2-needle perforations to remove the excess paper.

Finishing off:
Fold the card and insert a folded piece of rose-pink paper. Sew it into the bottom fold. Cut both ends of the card using a rule and a hobby knife.

of the card. Move the Pergamano paper and place it so the triangular part is connected correctly to the middle square.

With the gold Tinta, outline the drop-shaped figures.

Using white Tinta, outline the rest of the pansy and also the pollen.

In sepia Tinta, trace the three lower petals in the large pansy, the small petals within the large petals and also the small bud.

With violet Tinta, trace the top petals of the large pansy, the large petal in the small bud as well as the large bud, also the veins in the three lower petals.

With leaf green Tinta, trace the leaves and the stalks.

Move the Pergamano paper so the four hole combinations are placed in the right position. Using gold Tinta trace the drop-shaped figures. Now using white Tinta, trace the triangles.

Painting:
First application of Perga-Liner.

For the flowers and using PL A5 light blue, highlight the two top petals in flower and the large petal in the buds. For the two top petals in the flower and the large petal in the buds, shade more using PL A7 violet:

EXERCISE I: PANSIES

1. *The first layer of Perga-Liners.*

2. *The second layer of Perga-Liners.*

17 WORKING STAGES

The instructions that go with the designs in this book show one way of making the cards.

One of the enjoyable things about Parchment craft is that you are able to make cards in many different ways. From just one pattern, you can create many variations of a theme, each with a different aspect. Remember, each time you decide to prepare the card in a new way, you still have to use the following order for each technique.

1: Tracing.
2: Painting.
3: Dorsing.
4: Soft perforation.
5: Embossing.
6: Deep perforation.
7: Cutting.
8: Finishing off.

Exercise J, Christmas Card:

Tracing:

White Tinta: the candle, the wick, the flower petals and the large hearts.
Red Tinta: the bow.
Violet Tinta: the berries.
Leaf green Tinta: the spruce needles and the leaves.
Sepia Tinta: the flame, the stamens, the twig of the berries and the twig inside the fir.
Gold Tinta: the small hearts.

Painting:

Flowers: In the heart of the flower apply PL A20 light yellow. In the centre of the petals use PL A8 purple.
Berries: Apply PL A4 blue as first coat then PL A7 violet along the edge.
Flame: Put PL A20 in the lower part of flame and then PL A12 red in top of flame. Second coat PL A 11 orange.
Bow: PL A9 pink on the ends, and in the folds apply PL A8 purple for shading. Apply PL A7 under pre-

vious shading to accentuate the shadow. The second coat is then painted with PL A12 red.
The pine needles: Make fine lines with PL A13 light green and PL A14 green.
Leaves: For the darker shade use PL A16 olive green and for the second coat use PL A14 green.
Large hearts: a line outside the traced heart is painted with PL A12 red.

Perforating:

Perforate with the 4 needle tool where marked gently.

Embossing:

Candlelight: the lower part of the flame. Every twist is embossed along the outlines with the large ball tool.
Flowers: the centre and fine lines in the petals with the stylus. Emboss the petal with an oval movement so that it folds towards the card.
Berries: emboss using the small ball tool.
Leaves: gently emboss between the veins with the large ball.
The bow: Using the large ball tool, emboss to highlight the folds and also the ribbon ends.
The edge of the card: the small and the large hearts are embossed with the small ball tool, the dots between the perforations are made with the extra small ball tool.

Perforating:

Make deep perforations with the 4-needle tool where previously marked.

Cutting:

Cut the 4-hole combinations into crosses and slots. Cut the connections between the outer slits so the excess paper can be removed. The slits meet under the dot and also under the big heart.

Finishing off:

Fold the card and insert a folded piece of dark red paper. Remove the excess paper by cutting on the outside the edge of the design.

18 SHOPPING LIST

This list shows which materials are required to do the different exercises.

PERGAMANO PRODUCTS

Exercise A, Book mark:
Pergamano paper A4 (code 1481)
Tinta white 01T
Tinta gold 22T
Mapping pen (code 1420)
Embossing tool, small ball (code 1101)
Embossing pad, De Luxe (code 1413)
Paint/ink eraser (code 1423)

Exercise B, Card with flowers:
Embossing tool, fine stylus (code 1103)
White pencil (code 9202)

Repeating exercise A + B:
Dorso Crayons Box I (code 1440)

Exercise C, "Ship":
Embossing tool, large ball (code 1102)

Exercise D, "Stars":
Single needle tool (code 1104)
Felt embossing pad (code 1410)
Perga-Soft (code 1802)

Exercise E, 2 small gift tags:
3-needle tool (code 1108)
5-needle tool (code 1112)
Embossing tool, extra small ball (code 1107)
Perforation pad, "Excellent", A5 (code 1419)

Exercise F, "Mother's Day".
2-needle tool (code 1106)
Pergamano scissors, "Exclusive" (code 1131)
or:
Pergamano scissors, "Stainless" (code 1132)

OTHER PRODUCTS

Exercise A, Book Mark:
Tape
Scissors
Kitchen paper
Container for water

Exercise B, Card with flowers:
Coloured paper A4, 80 g
Needle & thread
Ruler
Paper clips

Repeating exercise A + B:
Lavender oil
A piece of material from a pair of tights.

Exercise C, "Ship":
No other materials

Exercise D, "Stars":
Dark cardboard

Exercise E, 2 small gift tags:
No other materials

Exercise F, "Mother's Day".
No other materials

Exercise G, Book Mark and card ("We've Moved").
4-needle tool (code 1105)

Exercise H, Butterflies.
Perga-Liners Box II (code 1451)

Exercise I, Pansy.
Tinta ink, sepia 12T
Tinta ink, violet 07T
Tinta ink, leaf green 10T

Exercise J, Christmas card.
Tinta ink, red 03T

Exercise G, Book Mark and card ("We've Moved").
No other materials

Exercise H, Butterflies.
No other materials

Exercise I, Pansy.
No other materials

Exercise J, Christmas card.
No other materials

NEW PERFORATING TECHNIQUE

Just when this book was ready for press we received information about a brand new perforating technique. As this technique can be considered to be a new basic technique, we decided to include it in this book.

Perforating with the help of a perforating template

The technique of making perforated decorations in parchment paper we have so far described in this book concerns the perforating with the help of a pattern with little dots placed underneath the parchment paper. The trick is to place the perforating tool on the dotted pattern as accurately as possible.

Now there is a new tool you can use during perforating: a perforating template with fine stainless steel netting. The sheet of parchment paper is placed on the template (drawing 1). A perforating tool is used to make little holes in the parchment paper. Due to the transparency of parchment paper the netting of the template is visible through the paper. You will have to perforate through the netting: the tool will go through the paper and will go into the meshes of the netting. Usually you will not insert the tool precisely in the centre of the meshes, but this will not be a problem. Due to its pointed tip the perforating tool will be guided towards the centre of the meshes. This way you

will be able to obtain a beautiful and regular perforation pattern.

Easy-Grid

The new Pergamano perforation template is called "Easy-Grid". The tool consists of a plastic frame with fine stainless steel netting with a mesh size of 1 mm. The size of the Easy-Grid is 25 cm x 18 cm. It is important that the netting of the template remains undamaged, therefore, if you store the template, do not place any heavy or sharp objects on it to avoid denting or bending the netting. It will be very hard to repair these damages, if at all possible.

Diamond perforating tool

There is a new perforating tool called "Diamond" for working with the Easy-Grid template. The tool has a square shaped tip (drawing 2). It is this square shape of the tip of this tool that made us think of the name "Diamond" tool. The shape of the tip corresponds with the shape and size of the meshes of the netting. During perforating you will have to twist the tool in the right position: if you can hardly twist it, the tool is in the right position. The tool has a white cap to protect the tip.

2

Perforating with the Easy-Grid

How do we use the new perforating template and perforating tool and what can we do with it?

This is how it is done, step by step:

1. Place your piece of work on the template, with the part of the pattern you want to perforate more or less in the middle of the Easy-Grid. Position the pattern in such a way that the hole pattern you want to make is parallel to the meshes of the netting.

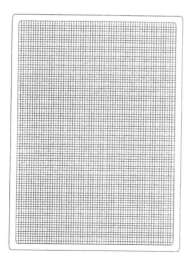

1

2. Attach your piece of work to the sides of the template with adhesive tape (drawing 3).

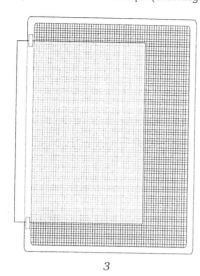

3

3. Take the Diamond perforating tool and place the tip above one of the meshes of the netting.
4. Gently twist the tool until its tip is parallel to the meshes of the netting.
5. Perforate the first hole and check whether the tool is indeed parallel to the meshes. By carefully wiggling the tool a bit you will feel whether a slight correction is necessary.
6. Hold the tool in this position and perforate a horizontal line of holes, going from left to right.
7. The tool should be held properly upright, to create regular perforations.
8. Perforate until you feel that the tool will not go in any deeper. After a bit of practise you will do this automatically.
9. Finish the horizontal row of holes, going from left to right.
10. Stay within the contours of the area you want to perforate. If the contour lines are not straight, you will have to see where you will have to add a hole or make one less to fill up the particular area as good as possible.

The perforated holes will be square, and the trick is to obtain a perforation pattern that is as regular as possible. This can be obtained by always holding the

tool properly upright and holding the square tip in line with the meshes of the netting.

There are two ways to perforate an area:
1. Filling up the pattern
2. Perforating in a certain pattern.

Filling up the pattern

This goes without saying: you will have to perforate in every mesh of the netting. Do not skip any of the meshes (picture 4).

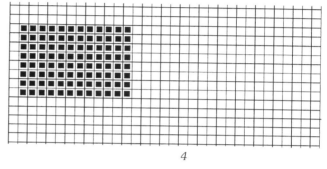

4

Perforating in a certain pattern

You will be making a certain pattern, which means that you will have to count, which may remind you of embroidery patterns, for example:
First row:
perforating 2 holes, skipping 2 holes, perforating 2 holes, skipping 2 holes
Second row:
perforating 2 holes, skipping 2 holes, perforating 2 holes, skipping 2 holes
Third row:
skipping 2 holes, perforating 2 holes, skipping 2 holes, perforating 2 holes
Fourth row:
skipping 2 holes, perforating 2 holes, skipping 2 holes, perforating 2 holes

This way you will create the perforation pattern of drawing 5.

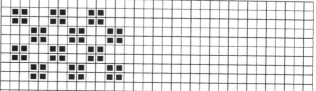

5

You can well imagine that you can perforate a pattern in many variations. You will have to pay attention though, once you have perforated on the wrong spot you will be stuck with an irreparable hole.

Brazilian method

This new method of perforating with the help of the Easy-Grid template originates from Brazil, and is therefore called the "Brazilian technique".

The story goes that this is the way the technique came into being:
A prisoner counted his days in jail by perforating holes in a sheet of paper with a nail. He made 10 holes in a horizontal row. Ten rows of 10 holes make 100 holes, or, for him, 100 days in jail; this way it was very easy for him to keep track of the number of days spent in jail. He discovered that with the help of a piece of netting he found in his cell, he could perforate the holes in nice, regular rows. The wife or girlfriend of this man heard about his technique and immediately thought of her hobby Parchment Craft.

Well, that's the way the Easy-Grid came into being, we heard.... It may or may not be true, but as soon as we have more information about it, we will let you know in one of our next Pergamano books.

An addition

The technique of perforating with the help of the Easy-Grid template is an addition to the already versatile hobby Parchment Craft. It does not replace any existing technique, such as perforating with the single-, 2-, 3-, 4-, 5-, or 7-needle perforating tool.

The new technique is very suitable for those people that have trouble seeing the ordinary perforation patterns or those who have trouble cutting crosses.

However, if you want you can cut the perforations into crosses. It is done the same way you cut the ordinary 4-hole perforations into crosses. The crosses will only be about 40% more apart from each other compared to the ordinary lace pattern. The crosses will also look a bit more flowery due to the shape of the perforated holes.

In future we will include the above-mentioned perforating technique in the new Pergamano patterns. It is a welcome addition to the already very versatile creative hobby Parchment Craft.

FURTHER INFORMATION

Since the introduction of the creative hobby Parchment Craft the company Marjo-Arte B.V. and I have trained a network of Registered Pergamano Tutors all over the world. These Tutors are qualified to give Parchment Craft courses for beginners, advanced students and children. You will also be able to follow courses on a special subject, like perforating & cutting, painting, working with Perga-Liner pencils etc.

Marjo-Arte has developed a training program to keep these Registered Pergamano Tutors up to date with the latest techniques and to bring their skills at the highest possible level.

Every Registered Pergamano Tutor is in possession of a Certificate and he or she will be happy to show it to you if so desired.

These Registered Pergamano Tutor are responsible for the way they conduct their as far as the teaching program, duration and materials used are concerned. A variation in course prizes may therefore occur.

You can write to Marjo-Arte B.V. (address at the end of this chapter) to obtain more information about the network of Registered Pergamano Tutors all over the world, the address of a Tutor in your neighbourhood etc.

Stichting Perga-Doe/Pergamano world

After the introduction of Parchment Craft in The Netherlands in 1990, the foundation "Stichting Perga-Doe" was established. The objectives of this foundation were: to make the Colombian folk art Parchment Craft known to the hobbyists and to promote this art form in a responsible manner. The main activity of the foundation is the issue of a magazine about Parchment Craft. The magazine is called **Perga-Doe** in the Netherlands and Belgium, and **Pergamano World** in every other country, and is being distributed 6 times a year.

In this magazine you will find:
* news about the hobby, techniques, materials and tools
* news about Parchment Craft fairs and manifestations all over the world
* patterns with working descriptions
* interesting stories or other information, tips, letters from subscribers, etc.

For further information you can write to:
Marjo-Arte B.V./Pergamano world
P.O. Box 2288
1180 EG Amstelveen
The Netherlands

or send a message to: www.Pergamano.com

ADDRESSES OF PERGAMANO IMPORTERS

Benelux: **Marjo-Arte B.V.**
P.O. Box 2288
1180 EG Amstelveen
The Netherlands
Fax: 020 6454181
www.pergamano.com

Singapore: **Art of Crafts**
160 Orchard Road
Singapore 238842
Fax: 235 9039

Japan: **CEO Corp.**
Rune Fujinomori 502
92-1 Mukaihatacyo Fukakusa
Fushimi-Ku, Kyoto 612
Tel./Fax: 075 645 4051

Canada/USA: **Exstasy Crafts**
Shannonville
Ontario KOK 3AO
Tel.: 613 968 7876

Denmark: **Fredensborg Indkobscentral**
Hojvangen 10
3480 Fredensborg
Fax: 48 48 4453/5144

Stenboden Skjern A/S
Svinget 22
6900 Skjern
Fax: 097 35 06 01

South Africa: **Perga-Kuns SA**
P.O. Box 3199
Kenmare 1745
Fax: 011 665-1934

New-Zealand: **R. & R. Pocock Limited**
Private Bag 3048
Rotorua
Fax: 07 348 9499

Canada/USA: **Exstasy Crafts**
Shannonville
Ontario KOK 3AO
Tel.: 613 968 7876

UK: **Pergamano UK Ltd.**
Eastfield Road,
Wellingborough
Northants NN8 1QX
Fax: 01933 274 099

Australia: **Rossdale PTY Ltd.**
Abbotsford
P.O. Box 222
Victoria, 3067
Fax: 03 9482 3874